RESOLVE
POEMS

RESOLVE

NYAH VANTERPOOL

POEMS

Copyright © 2021 by Nyah Vanterpool
www.NyahVanterpool.com

All rights reserved. This book or any portion thereof may not be reproduced or used in any manner whatsoever without the express written permission of the publisher except for the use of brief quotations in a book review.

Printed in the United States of America

First Printing, 2021

ISBN 978-1-7368233-1-6 (paperback)
ISBN 978-1-7368233-6-1 (ebook)

Library of Congress Control Number 2021906930

Rising Moon Creatives
St. Louis, MO
www.RisingMoonCreatives.com

Cover Design, Editing, & Publication by Rising Moon Creatives

Dedicated to my wife, Allison, whose support and encouragement made this book possible.

Contents

Introduction	1
About the Author	5
Timber	6
Dreaming	8
Why	9
Confronting	11
Patriotism	12
Assimilation	14
Depletion	15
Exile	16
Volcanic	17
Onward to Victory	18
Charge	20
Colonization	21
Takun Olum	22
Truth is Truth	23
Wayward Ways	24
Cognitive Load	26
Virtues	27
Delegation	28
Brutality	29
Pain Points	30
Lost Generation	31
F.O.M.O.	32
Luke 7:31	35
Duty Bound	36
Commitment	38

Election Season	39
A c k n o w l e d g i n g	41
Atonement	42
Unapologetically White	43
Self Assessment	44
Crying Song	45
Detainment	46
Money Motivated	47
Fear Based Leadership	48
Boomers	49
Failure	50
Peace	51
Wait For It	52
Power	53
Anti-Racism	54
Rise	56
Petition	58
Resilience	59
Distrust	60
Positive Progress	61
U n i t i n g	63
Never Again	64
Disruption	65
Unified Agenda	66
Emancipation	67
Cause & Effect	68
Mortality	69
Immemorial	70

Longings	71
Legacy	72
Reincarnation	73
To Do List	74
Language Games	75
Regeneration	76
Hope	77
Divine Intentions	78
Reparations	79
A c t i v a t i n g	81
Return to Paradise	82
Apple Seeds	83
Fruits of Peace	84
Community	85
Revolutionary	86
Fruits of Fear	87
Reward Assessment	88
Pros & Cons	90
Best Bets	91
Direct Action	92
Lots	93
Possibilities	94
Home	95
Happy Joy	96
Peacekeeping	98
Rules of Engagement	99
Swag	100
Grace	101
COVID Times	103

Resurrection	103
Blessings	104
R.A.I.N.	106
Love	107
Flow	108
Ready	109
Set	110
Slow Going	111
Go	112
Let Go	113
Redemption Song	114

Introduction

This collection of poems reflects upon the years between 2016 and 2021. This time was marked by the election of Donald Trump to the office of President. He won office by vowing to "build a wall," "drain the swamp," and generally, "Make America Great Again." President Trump's reliably callous treatment of race- and human-relations ensured that news and social media would be consistently awful.

During these years, all forms of media were flooded with incidents of police wielding undue force, brutalizing, degrading and killing black and brown people. Millions of guns continued to be sold each year with sales rocketing every time there was a school shooting or another cause for national alarm. Children labelled "illegal immigrants" were interned at the Mexican border.

While the number of racist white massecurists raged across the nation - in churches, schools, theaters, and elsewhere - Muslims were banned from entering the United States because they were perceived to be terrorists. We hated the people and health of our world. We pulled out of the Paris climate accords. We pulled out of the World Health Organization during the start of a global pandemic. We insulted international and democratic allies. We lauded authoritarians and dictators.

Our dissents became riotous. We burned cities. We stormed the capital. We were vocal and visual about our distrust of Democrats and Republicans alike. Some were Proud Boys and Girls. Some were Anti-Fascists. Separate but together, we tacitly agreed to hate "the Establishment" enough to wage a violent culture war. Separate but together, we devoutly hated the government, the other party, and the politicians who make it all possible.

This time was marked by dedicated resistance. On one side, an alternative right-wing of patriots demanded that Western white ways remain dominant. On the other side, a collective camped under the banner of "Black Lives Matter" resolved to remedy racism and repair the poverty that has been caused by 400 years of discriminatory practices. Protestors around the world insisted they would not be choked by the hands of ignorance or bound by the chains of hate. On each side, young people insisted that change be made now.

Nyah Vanterpool's poetry collection Resolve aims to challenge contemporary perspectives around race, American identity, and disunity. Vanterpool offers a portrait of a mixed black man reconciling the promise of the American dream with the reality of America's toxicity and legacy of violent oppression. Vanterpool's poetry joins together a denouncement of hate, racism, and American exceptionalism with a unifying call to peace, hope, forgiveness, and repair. Poems pull at the tension of hope and fear, and the duality of feeling both American and other. Resolve represents a restless wish for racism to end.

About the Author

Timber

My hands are the surest reminder of my race.
The color of my skin is a gradient of light brown.
At any time, I am like a finely finished wood grain
with shades that fade
into and out of smooth brownness.

As far as blackness goes,
I am a light skinned
tourist
                     of the purest line.

As far as whiteness goes,
I am black
but the kind of black
that is thought of as "fine."

My winter fingers count the months
until my skin darkens;
the shallow greenish blue veins
        that unveil a history of colorism
        and colonized prisons
are concealed by the summer sun.

The white of my thighs even in tone
matching the tenor of my timber hues.

Resolve

My brown body is a beautiful muse.

My hands cruise through racial shifts
with the flip of a wrist.

Brown back, white palms
holding alms in solidarity.
Within my body's polarity
there is good news.

You get to choose
to see me
        as I am.

Dreaming

I have a dream that one day
little black boys and little black girls
will be able to feel seen
and valued in this world
        that easily overlooks them,
        locks them up,
        and over-crooks them.

I have a dream that one day
        the mountaintops
        will stop growing taller,
        that this next step
will see us arrive
at peak peace.

I have a dream
        that seems too simple:
        freedom for all
to roam and settle
        these many lands
in pursuit of a good life.

I have a dream that we all will know
a life full of color.

I have a dream that, one day, we together
will end racism, penury, and the memory of apathy
        found in the land of the free and home of the brave.

Why

America, I went down
to your rivers to pray
and was taken by your waters.

I did not float.

I descended
into your depths rung by rung
to find our descendants
hung, waiting for peace
and the penance of their persecutors.

You would ask me to salute
these flags, or drown
and be dragged by the tides?

I wish for us to wade,
be baptized
and reborn into a new land
with new ways,
where all our ancestors
are raised
from these drifting waves.

Confronting

Patriotism

America, must we thank you
for this amnesia?

Your memories hide.

How many Americans were killed
while the poet penciled this poem?

How many citizens and civilians
were left without homes?

How many deaths will it take
to repair Our Founding Fathers' mistakes?

For which and whose sake?

What's the price we are willing to pay
        to hunt an American Eagle?
                A beagle?
                A beetle?
                An Arab?
                A Talib?
                A criminal?
                A bad guy?
                A villain?

Who dares
to test these red, white, and blue angels?

Resolve

Are we good Yankee Doodlers with dandy ways,
or will there soon come a day
we tire and reply "You're fired,

Fear?" Fear
for the end of an age
is near.

Let a new epoch cheer.

"Fall Flags.
Hold not fast
to these towering poles.

Lay and decay
in the earth
to remember our shared beginning.

Not only are you a false god, an idol
of no good substance, you are
a hypocrite, Flag,
      an unfulfilled promise,
      a word without action,
      a broken pledge,
      a rejected transaction."

To be free and to be freed
we must eventually flee
from our longing
to belong to a history
that never happened.

Assimilation

America, where have the patriots gone marching? Down
the black, tarred road -
puffing smoke, poisonous emissions;
herding hope, a merchandising mission;
selling Coke, for the commissions -

we tread.
America, we make cavemen into catatonic cravers;
neighbors with borders;
love, with strict orders and request forms.

America, our norms are not charming.
A citizen army is not disarming.
It's alarming how scared we are
of our brothers and sisters,
our misses and misters.
Our blisters hurt
from walking
so far, stocking
up scars,
chalking hate up to "Life's hard,"
taking out frustrations at bars,
celebrating victory every night
with the stars
on TV
dancing, romancing us
to remember

the American opiate awaits
but never satiates.

Depletion

Ego experienced
a depletion event
of elite proportions
taking place just north of emptiness
an abortion of the one and only holy I
a sum of you your Self
and everything else you claim
to own and know, gone,
all in one minor key: *me me me*.

Exile

Humanity keeps
demanding we
make another calamity.

While free land
is sold and the sea
is mined for black gold,

our time is told
       to grow old
             and unbothered

by the things we bottle up
by the stuff we throw away
by the number of years

   we waste on decay-
   -ing the essence
   of where we began:

               the sea,
               the land,
                    roaming free,
                    running wild,

honoring the earth as the mother
and we, the child.

Volcanic

Dense, mixed and made up in a molten core
we bellow out and roar through the atmosphere.

We push the wind
to claim ourselves more dangerous than chaos.

We spit sulfur that sends smoke
signaling the story of ages.

We saunter while scorching petals and plants.
Our raging fire slides through
simmering mammals, lizards, and ants.

We cannot resist the temptation to burn
               every solid and hollow thing.

Our power promises to return
everything to the rock of origins.

Onward to Victory

How far can anyone see?

The only competition
that makes good sense
is how to best be free
and keep our white picket fence.

What defense does peace take
when others forsake
a sacred duty?

What riches are worth mining and looting?

Who, if anyone, is ever worth shooting,
or whipping, or chaining, or jailing, or
God, I hope not, impaling?

To whom are you mailing a love letter?

What are you doing now to get better?

Have you tried cool air near a fiery place;
spiced rum and a sweater;
drums during rainy weather;
a therapist named Heath or Heather?

Resolve

Nah.

You haven't
and likely won't.

You wish
you knew better.
You don't

stop. Because
this is hard,

continue
the charge.

Charge

Ramble all you want
with an American flag.

Wave it to the stars
and don't forget to brag.

Hold your guitars near.
Strum those chords.

Praise to the heavens
whoever your lords, and

don't forget your gourds

for the floods of change are coming.

The waves are fast moving,

running for peace.

We are coming for peace.

Colonization

Greed is our decadent shelter,
our solitary society,
our well developed
economic plans
supporting
supply and demand,
rights over man,
and fights over land
settled by wars on [fill in the blank]
as the command.

Takun Olum

A kettle of rum
gave us the sum
of a grave digging
economy. Enslavement
was a harmonious chord
to white people
who yet progress
by the tip of the Ford,
dollar, and plastic bottle.

Truth is Truth

This cotton
blanketing us
and our history
is just a scary story
called American glory.

Pour another cup
of no hope
for us dopes.

Sip the sin
we condone and
own with every
fiber of our clothes
and tax dollars.

Life,
an ancient sacrament,
is yet sacrificed
for cents
and tribal sentiments.

We men, minted by our metal
and might, mean wealth and well
when we usher Hell by selling
war and imprisonment,
enslavement and poverty,
technology and temples
made to be monumental-
-ly inequitable.

Wayward Ways

Democracy is a nice notion
unless you're
a poor person,
black person,
motherless child,
fatherless son,
made a mistake,
to the church we must run.

Beautiful is our bureaucracy,
a paper inspired kakistocracy,
legalistic
like broccoli.

American meritocracy can suck my -balls:
basket-, foot-, meat-, and all.

Our colorful flesh will mesh well
when we reverse this spell
called idiocracy. Attacks on reason

make one miss the aristocracy;
yearn for the fresh revolutionary air
of daring writers
who scribble about

freedom and truth.
History's fighters

Resolve

wield a pen as mightier
than a sword,
but, good Lord,
we have long ignored
books and bibles,
replaced by screens,
tribal terrors, and storybook errors.

This oblong, prolonged ministry of madness
administers debt and death,
calls penury fair and says "We will fare well."

Yet, somehow, our rulers
will wonder how we ended in Hell.

Cognitive Load

Now what?

Oh no.

My brain
overloads.

My heart
explodes.

My will moves
fearfully slow.

My desire wishes
to move fast.

My hope sets
on making impact.

My reality ties
to needing cash.

In the end,
I can only do
this much.

The rest
gets chalked up
to such and such.

Virtues

By a tree, we sat and sang of Joy.
It was sorrowful.
Joy was crying.

To the sun, we sat and sang of Hope.
It was sorrowful.
Hope was dying.

By the lake, we sat and sang of Beauty.
It was sorrowful.
Beauty was buying.

To the flowers, we sat and sang of Wisdom.
It was sorrowful.
Wisdom was lying.

In this wilderness, we only found thorns
pricking our flesh, spilling the blood of regrets
for letting it all come to this.

Delegation

Following fast facts
and vague orders

that whip around
liminal borders,

while walking on
slippery ground,

reading fog
covered signs,

clear directions
are hard to mine.

Brutality

Ignorance is
        caring not to cover the tracks and traces,
not looking back
        at the facts that face us
        or the faces behind facts,
        taxes, or ruthless attacks.

Ignorance happily lets you bleed,
        and does not believe
your storied scars.

Ignorance keeps you
behind bars,
        never to be free,
        never to see reality
        beyond the prison.

Pain Points

These bodies feel soft.
These brains fall feeble.

These futures appear faint.
These pasts play sequels.

These paths are broken.
These wheels are spinning.

These gears are stuck.
What luck! The breaking point is beginning.

Lost Generation

Are we a lost generation,
      a weed tumbling
          across a dusty prairie?

Are we wandering
      a desert without mana?

Are we searching for a promised land,
      while fighting faith?

Are we the slaves escaping,
      or perhaps,
the Pharaoh's soldiers
      drowning in the Red Sea?

Are we free to be anything good
or bound to be everything bad?

Are we the start of something special,
something mad in between,
or something unholy ushering the end of being?

F.O.M.O.

It is mysterious.
This life is serious.

To not know that
you must be delirious.

Marry up.
Merry up.

Hurry fast
before you're buried

up in those mistakes.
Or is this fate?

Is it too late
to be one of the greats?

When you die
will you wonder why
you never knew holding
a child who cried?

And what of your life?
Did you love your wife?
Did you travel the world,
learning to play flute or fife?

Did you see that show?
Did you get to go?
Did you tattoo your legs,
pierce your tongue or nose?

Resolve

And what of those?
And what of these?

Did you say please,
thank you to your knees
and the cool wintry breeze?

Did you dunk it once?
Did you make it twice?
Did you learn to make sushi
with spicy tuna and rice?

Were you nice enough?
Were you kind yet tough?
Were you strong through
all those times that got rough?

Did you play outside?
Did you learn to glide?
Did you find that person
with whom you choose
to confide

your everything?
It is everything.

Look at those dreams
quickly severing.

Can you get them back?
Have you found the map?

Might I recommend you
retrace your tracks
to Level 1?

Maybe what you should do
is go for a run.

Be fresh and tan.
Play Wheel of Fortune.
Lead sing in a band.
Own lots of land.
Own lots of money too.
Buy a spaceship.
Turn it into a zoo.

Anchor on the news.
Buy a guitar.
Pick away the blues
in a garage
or maybe a bar.

Now, how will you choose?
Which way will you charge?
Will you venture a way that is easy
or struggle doing something hard?

Luke 7:31

We are like constipation,
full of waste and stuck with it,
pushing for change,
impatiently waiting,
counting the days
until the old gut is emptied,
flushed but not forgotten,
praying for relief,
for this rotten time to be over.

Duty Bound

We dreamers must yet dream.
We healers must yet heal.
We teachers must yet teach
to each their own
        horrifying truths.
In this nation we bemoan good graces,
        pay to patrol black faces,
        erase Muslims from our spaces,
        and raise the Confederacy on pedestals,
while discounting the devastating toll of inaction.

Leaders, dissolve these factions.
Repair hate down to the transaction.

Our houses too big.
Our taxes too small.
Our pleasures too plenty.
Spend cents on suffering,
billions on cops and malls.

Is this the end as we know it?
Is there no bridge to mend;
no moral arch to bend?

Knowledge is where this all began.
        a span of x number of years
        with "WHY?" number of deaths
        divided by z number of slaves,
        and we get the funkiest
        formula for progress.

Account for the culture war multiplier,
        the climate deniers, and the conspirators

Resolve

to get your axis. Watch the battle between
Christians and Catholics versus Muslims and all others.

It's been a white supremacy rhyme
       about a black on black crime
       told by a Confederacy
that reminds you
of alternative facts
       made to cover for lies.

These were brown ropes around black necks
       swinging from green trees,
             a red December christened
             with cotton snowflakes,
                   bloodied hands, bloodied backs,
starving families and all of that
               depraved stuff
               we set on fire
               to forget.

Children born to our demon lands
covet the power of supply and demand
where human lives can be damned
for dollars and false fears.

My dears, subtract evil actions,
       add good taxes,
then get that love fraction on.

All we ever needed to do was care
for our neighbors and sing songs.

Commitment

Burn doubt.

Unburden yourself from doubt.

Untangle doubt.

Undo nothing.

Own the truth, consequences,
risks, and rewards
in an ever-towards devotion

to do better
together.

Election Season

Roll this numbered dice.

Step this direction.

Open the door to paradise
or pandora
with this next election.

Acknowledging

Atonement

It's a tone meant
for the hell bent
and the hard of hearing,
whose hearts are like stones
thrown at the head of peace,

whose words are like a venous bite
laced with an unholy hate,
whose thoughts are wasted
on greed and complacency
with pride acted faithlessly

in stars and stripes
that promise equality,

that demand liberation,
that hail a nation
established under
a compassionate God
who weeps for the lost.

Unapologetically White

That never happened,
        and if it did,
            it wasn't me.
That's not my problem.
          We're Americans.
          You and I are free.

Get over it.
Do something about it.
Change your ways.
Do not touch my taxes,
        or with my vote,
           require me to pay.

You said it wrong.
You have no right.
You disrespected the flag
        and picked a fight.

You had it coming.
It's just your fault.
Quit making excuses.
Maybe, exalt God? Instead
        try prayer.

        See? There,
there. I care.
        Plus,
        I have a black friend.

Self-Assessment

What then
when the mirror looks back
to ask:

"Why
aren't you fuller
in spirit than me?

Why
are you looking
at and for me
to fill you up?"

Crying Song

All those slaves died.

Shut up about it already.

MLK parted the red seas,
and Americans are free.

Quit making me think
of slavery.

Quit asking me
to turn my head
from our founding bravery.

We were brave, weren't we?

Detainment

Our mind can be freed.

Our bodies are always confined,

bound to age,

> wage,

> nature,

> nation,

> and the times.

Money Motivated

These
days
got
me
        feeling
        like
        I'm
        falling
in
love
with
class
and
capturing
that
cash
        fast.

Fear Based Leadership

Stand alert,
> watch steady,

count these meals,
> and guard our pennies.

Guard our cars.
Guard our ground.
Guard the things
> we purchased or found.

> Remember to

load your gun,
lift your safety,
and get ready for some fun times
> conquering our fears
> and protecting our stuff.

Boomers

Hey baby.
How are you doing?

Do you like money and cars?
Smokey billiards and bars?

If so, let's get to screwing
this and the next
seven generations over
while we rover my muscled car

to get some McDonald's fries
and bond over Hollywood lies
while we disguise our politics.

Failure

You got hit with
    a joy seizure,

    a displeasure center
    entered without a choice,

a thought
    stabbing the soul
    out of control,

    settled
    everywhere
    that hurts,

    a moment
    to let go,

    a mention
    that shakes
    and breaks
    the foundation
    of everything
    you've known
    and owned
    in the old
    version of zen

    expecting you
to wash,
rinse,
repeat,
and try again.

Peace

Scatter Black Lives Matter.

Shatter Antifa.

Shoot people
to protect property.

Watch from home
eating pizza.

Cheer on the police
for "doing their duty."

Ignore the deep issues
because some folks are looting.

Wait for It

Soon
all will be revealed.

Yet,

your path will not become clear.

Your flow will not go smoothly.

Your destiny will halt before indecision.

Your will shall hesitate.

You will intuit a wrong direction.

You will promote a poorly thought predilection.

You will make a selection for better and for worse.

Regardless of the size and scope of
your purse and position,

your mission will always be
to survive and overcome

this day and the next.
When you pray for the best of luck,
trust that such will follow.

Power

Whites took black and brown lives.
Whites took black and brown lands.
Whites took black and brown culture
while saying "be damned
or be saved,
       if you behave
we will allow you to live
in the home of the Braves."

Hence, if you ask the Sioux
"Who should rule?"
They likely will not answer
"That righteous white crew."

Let's be clear.
Western society is a solution
       some find differently dear.

Listen here.
There are those whose simple wish
is to peacefully co-exist
       without catering
       to how much the tax-man gets
because he forgets
       those war-time debts,
       those treacherous betrayals
            committed with little regret.

The Western table is set.
The Western bet is rigged.
Whites made it best
to impoverish
black and brown kids.

Anti-Racism

All people matter,
including the blacks,
the browns,

                              the wetbacks
                              we wished would drown
                              in the Rio Grand
                              before entering this land.

                              Those sand niggers
                              should dust off their shoes,
                              or better yet,
                              go back to the Middle East.

                              Those moon crickets
                              should quiet down.
                              Quit making a mess
                              of our history.

There is no mystery.

We are Americans,
        proud and a bit arrogant,
        loud and spirited.

So just

Resolve

take it in the ear.

Take it to the polls.

Take it up with the police
and those of us who own guns.

We were founded free and continue to be
that. Anything else said is anti-fact backed by Antifa.

And in case you forgot:
#AllLivesMatter #BlueLivesMatter. Of course,

                                        non-white lives matter too,
                                        as well as animals we like
                                        to keep in the zoo.

Rise

We left the grave. Behind us
lies every precious moment.

Let the lessons take.

We have a mission:
to give rise.

We have glorious visions, called life, love, and living
to give rise.

We read these next words.
We take this next breadth and
give rise. Once more,

make no quarter for misery.
Mine the mystery to be made rich.

Give rise for this
is no place or time for endings.

Give rise to wiping away weariness.
No despising. No revising.
Survive on the morsels of these many moments
that crawl with innocence.

Be made full by every emotion and cling to none.

We are at home, one body, one temple.

Lay still and give thanks.

Resolve

Here, we say "Good day, Fear.
We bid you farewell.
Be gone spirits of Hell.

We shall visit you no more in the shadows.
We shall not let our deep souls be shallowed
one shovel at a time.

We shall not tip our heads,
topple our crowns,
or set down our chalice
for any less than divine intervention.

We are royalty, and you, Fear, are placed in detention."

Here's chalk.
No talking.
Repeat these blessings.
No balking.

"**We are good and mighty**,"
we say. We all write.

Petition

Let's go back
to the good old days,
those traditional ways,
before we were attacked
by the blacks and browns.

Remember back when
the towns were built up,
not burnt down and graffitied?

Remember back when
every decision was sound?

Remember back when we had integrity
and were not at odds with our fellows?

Remember back when people from all walks of life
would pass by saying "Hello, good morning?"

Those rich old times seem long gone,
a fantasy, now only remembered in song.

Almost as if it never happened,
like it was all a dream.

Resilience

Shed two tears
in a bucket.

Dry out
in the warm sun.

Say "I don't know
the answer.

I did it wrong on the first time;
now I'm a second chancer."

Grow
thicker skin,
a wider grin,
a glowing spirit within
that shines from shoes to chin

then

proudly begin again.

Distrust

One foot in Heaven.

One foot in Hell.

The promise of walking
through this life
is a spell

they sell.

Will you buy
the poisons
or the elixirs,

sourced from the truth-tellers
or the tricksters?

Positive Progress

Bonded to the past,
reconciling becomes our task,
moving towards a chance
to sing a new song
that echoes longer
than generations can account.

That history becomes
a reminder to move forward.

What's ahead is
a good reason
to choose loving life and living
now. For "now"
is the only time we can share.
The rest is a memory to cherish.
Before we perish,
monumentalize the experience
in however it felt at the time.

Here now,
step forward.

Clap your hands.

Stomp your feet.

Repeat this motion
as many times as it takes
to not feel defeated
by the way you say
"We are going to be
okay."

Uniting

Never Again

That thing, that destruction,
those mistakes, those instructions,
these fears, these eruptions
these years of Greed's conduction;

that warring, that hate,
that thinking that this can wait;
that vote left unfulfilled,
those people that person killed;

our silence, our screams,
our broken promises, our fiends;
such terrors, such horrors,
so many errors, so many borders,

let us be. Let us be.
Let us humans roam wholly free.
Take these taxes. Take these tithes.
Purchase peace. Save some lives.

Do no harm. Pray no evil.
Set slaves free. Help the feeble.
Live on less. Love lots more.
Build community like it's a chore.

Read a book. Attend a meeting.
Greet a stranger. Make some meaning.
Maybe then, why not now,
that someday will be found.

Disruption

I knew a new practice of dreaming,

      living now on the prowl,
a prophecy of somehow

                    loving despite
a divisive scenario,
apt to fail but for the alternative,

a prevailing wisdom,
      not bought but taught,

spoken in the disruption of peace,
a defiant piece of us,

as quiet and resolute as can be,

keeping going, knowing

      and showing love
to these transgressors.

Unified Agenda

Our nest rests
on a jagged cliff edge.

We must pledge to rock
gently, to huddle
for warmth,
to learn to be fearless
when we leap
to fly south for the winter.

Emancipation

What justice do we seek
in these cantankerous times?

What glory do we pursue
while walking the party line?

What hope do we fulfill
with each judgment and action?

What fate do we seal
battling with many factions?

At this dark hour,
before our pride goes before the fall,
whose liberation are we exacting
if anyone's at all?

Cause & Effect

Could it be that we are out of touch
    with the reality of cause and effect,

that we are caught chasing a curving path,
    fearing downslopes and plateaus,
    chasing exponential growth and predictable math

that allows us to mine and maybe master uncertainty,
    tame the chaos,
    make and win the playoffs,

despite the risks,
    because of the mismeasured rewards,
    because of a twisted definition of land-
    -lord, ownership, and wealth?

Mortality

Death is the sea of life
        eroding Earth,
carving mountains and canyons
        into our cheeks,
promising that our waking soul
        was put to good use
        and our decaying legacy
will yet be mined for its treasures.

Immemorial

History is
        a portal to nowhere
        we really know,
                save for photos,
                third eye feelings,
                and scriptural revealings.

That time
        is an elusive dream,
yet to be fulfilled,
        or a nightmare
        terrorizing today.

Which past will you grasp?

Which future will you present?

Longings

Yesterday is a memory
to be replete with joy.

Today is a victory
to be repeated.
Enjoy.

Tomorrow is a story
we hope not to destroy.

Now is a time for glory
we intend to employ.

Legacy

Ancestry pulls us into
               a collective dimension;
               a descension
               into descendancy,
a past-present-future interdependency;
               a purposefully planted mending tree
that knows little of our counting
down the seconds, seeds,
and centuries;
               an inheritance of penury;
               a never-ending injury;
               a bruised lemon
                              yet fit for aide
                              that we must spade
                              into a new generation
                              of good fruits.

Reincarnation

People
are inextricably equal.

Whether good or evil
we all share the same sequel.

Death is not merely medieval,
heavenly, hellish, or peaceful.

For some death is a "Pardon me
from this hardened world."

For others, death is an execution.

For some unnamed,
death is a Final Solution.

Pause.

If we all were to die today
our lives would live on
beyond decay,
recycled into dirt and clay.
Save for our pollution,

we are all rebirthed in the earth's evolution.

To Do List

And do not forget the pieces you left behind
on the trail you traveled in a hope to find
an answer to a question that is just as confusing
as the location of the pieces you seem to keep losing.

And do not forget to heal yourself first
before seeking repentance with those you hurt worst,
for your mind must find a place more stable
away from the disservice of what formerly enabled.

And do not forget to trace your steps to the past
to catch the stones you once wrongly cast,
and repair the bridge you chose to shatter
breaking ties with the life that yester had mattered.

And do not forget to continually grow
persistently trying although you might not know
the place where the pieces will perfectly fit
because though incomplete, your life is still a gift.

Language Games

Alabamans and Georgians
got a lot alike.

Those Prairie-born, don't you know,
pack a real fight.

About the DMV
they're keeping it real.

All the places you will go
they express
how they feel,
what they think,
who they are
beyond the brink,

singing in many native tongues,
all in one resounding chorus,
calling for peace and prosperity
for their people.

Regeneration

Historical distortions,
restore them.
                      Reform conflicting facts.
                      Make them a myth.
                      Keep them honorably inexact.

                                            Quibble.
                                           Be over them.
                                           Take lessons
                                           and tact.

                                           Laugh at,
                                           shy from,
                                           get lost in
                                           the acts.

Maximize the struggle
when telling the story
of how we huddled
and handled hope.

Hope

Celebrate hope,
a dope that stokes potential,
takes us to peace from feeling mental
or lost,
dismally dancing,
weighing the world's
many costs.

"Who's the boss?" You hear
hope flings fear far away.

The nightmares no longer scare.

This maze of life gets solved with magic.

Souls stir against what's tragic
because hope is a trace advantage,
a point forward,
a lighthouse to shore,
a simple chore:
to believe now
is our time
to overcome
this thing.

Divine Intentions

Let us care
      for the sick in body,
      for the sick in spirit,
      for the ailing city and its servants,
      for the works of the deacons.

Let us seek
      miracles of healing,
      miracles of provisions,
      miracles of awakening,
      miracles of courage.

Let us discern
      the stirring of our own souls,
      the weakness of our own doubts,
      the direction of our own convictions,
      the stillness of our own untroubled waters.

Let us now live, and let go
as we row alone and together
along the way of life.

Reparations

What would Jesus do?
I ask the question of Lady Justice too?

Use judgment, scales, and/or rules?
Choose to suffer and forgive fools?

Muse about sinful snakes,
floating gardens and mystic gates?

Would either
earnestly deliberate what is good

for Heaven's and humans' sake?
Maybe they would

face facts free from fiction, falsities, and fakes?
Trace acts through to the origin of causal and colossal mistakes?

Might they bother to debate, or
just wait to cast a verdict, levy a charge,

weigh possible costs and punishments
to determine how large the reparations?

Activating

Return to Paradise

We went the long way, astray. To be okay
pray we reshape the clay
by molding our movements with meaning.

Set the wheel to motion.
Steady the erosion of self.

Hold on to home,
a place always known,
a sanctuary always owned,
a garden always grown,
a sacred dwelling.

Fall at the foot of Mt. Sinai -
head above denial,
heart on trial,
soul seeking revival -
and drink this vial of truth.

Let us be together. Here
in relationship with grace
is where we might be revealed
in a good faith response.

Go now.
Do something
holy.

Apple Seeds

Forgive the old ways
for some day
all will be forgotten.

However ripe or rotten,
however far fallen from the tree,
these seeds are good for sewing
another bushel of apples.

Fruits of Peace

The fruits of peace are joy.
The fruits of joy are freedoms.
The fruits of freedoms are (w)holiness.
The fruits of (w)holiness are hope.
The fruits of hope are wisdom.
The fruits of wisdom are gladness.
The fruits of gladness are goodness.
The fruits of goodness are virtues.
The fruits of virtues are righteousness.
With righteousness, we find resolve.
With resolve, we find confidence.
With confidence, we find and know commitment.
In loving commitment, we better know compassion.
    Compassion begets empathy.
    Empathy calls for unity.
    Unity requires sacrifice.
    Sacrifice ennobles relationships.
Relationships are the foundation of community.

Community

These neighbors are

> your cavalry,
> your reinforcements,
>
> ready to assemble,
> willing to charge
>
> to take a stand
> by your side
>
> defending your keep-
> -sakes and treasures

valuable beyond measure,
seeing you through
seasons of pain and pleasure.

Revolutionary

Storm the temple.

Topple tables.

Combat merchant fables.

Label haters.

Label liars.

Offer allegoried gifts
to deniers.
        To make their plight lighter

raise a prayer
to the open ceiling

then return to the streets
carrying that righteous feeling.

Fruits of Fear

The fruits of fear are hate.
The fruits of hate are violence.
The fruits of violence are pain.
The fruits of pain are suffering.
The fruits of suffering are struggle.
The fruits of struggle are overcoming
       the temptation to retaliate.

Reward Assessment

Before we set our eyes
to the stars beyond
these skies, let us remember:

Our Earth has yet to sing.
We have yet to wear leaves.
We have yet to dance in the trees.
We have yet to plant seeds that don't freeze.
We have yet to regenerate the seas

because

we are yet infants in this world.
We twirl together in harmony and discord.
We set life and liberty to motion with notions and swords.
We cater to our tastes from socks to awards.

We are overflowing with inventive zeal.
We are a magical and mysterious blip in feel and time.
We are unbounded earthly beings;
others like us, we cannot find.

We possess might
to manifest dreams and craft minds
that make destinies through soulful decisions.

We determine the course by answering
who and what do we hold in admiration and derision?

Resolve

When is our love and hate worth giving?

What shall we hope for and wish to doom?
How shall we shine before and after the high noon sun?

Towards what moon shall we howl, walk, run?

How shall we sculpt the dirt
and design the day?

Over what are we God,
if even the clay?

Pros & Cons

Fear is a fiction we fend off.
Hope is a fantasy we lean into.

Small and big possibilities,
all pursued the same,

with a lack of answers,
with many steps in a game.

Best Bets

  Potion your portion;
be a miracle in motion,

    spiritual in notion,
    an ocean of prayer,

    levity, courage, and quality of care,
    a simple swear

    sent there
    in a daring guess.

  Drink in the air
then brave your best bets.

Direct Action

Head up the hill,
creating momentum
to leap with a purpose

                                                              to take flight

                                      or glide

                            through

                  the canyon,
        across the plateau,
over the peak,
    under the water,
           down the street,
                      near the valley forged
                by pioneers
          who
      survived
to tell
the story.

Lots

This life is a lot.

This lot is all we got.

Pick a plot.

Purchase and plant seeds.

Tend to the weeds.

Serve our basic needs,
and be nice.

If not, think twice.

Give thanks to the rice,
and do the next thing

haphazardly, ready to tell the tale
of how we rose

after we failed
at growing
tulips this spring.

Possibilities

Float high
enough to look down on the cars,
up at the stars,
seeing Mars, birds, and rivers.
In a new light,

suspend here.

Depend only on this air
we share.

Though vertical,
sense no vertigo.

Feel no fear.
Think, "Oh dear,

how to steer
this cloud
on which
we ride?"

Home

Home is where the birds chirp,
where we still and steal glances,
where time talks and ticks matter not.

What is kept at home
is sacred.

Who is allowed in
is a choice.

For this reason
we portion our voice
with compassionate consideration.

Frustrations,
elations, and all
that which we are
belongs here at home.

Happy Joy

Happiness is a fly fleeing.
Joy is an anchor in the fresh mountain air.

Breathing and eating fine food is fleeting too.
Joy is a study held at noon.

Joy is laughter followed by smiles.
Happiness is being wild.

Happiness is walking miles in a calming rain,
carrying the elements in your fabric, skin, bones, and brain.
Joy is remembering that lightning is an ill-tempered chaos,
a concert of thunder and gentler beats.

Happiness is driving down the streets in a car.
Joy is knowing all that carried you even this far.

Happiness is in the going.
Joy is in the growing.

Happiness is showing off.
Joy is caring for the many costs.

Happiness is smoking weed.
Joy is planting seeds.

Happiness is a lover's touch.
Joy is a heart- and soul-bound trust.

Happiness is scooping the crust from the sandy shore.
Joy shoots straight from the core.

Resolve

Happiness molds minutes.
Joy sculpts lifetimes.

Happiness flails in the face of grief.
Joy prevails with earnest belief.

Happiness is a futuristic inspection.
Joy is living present and in quiet reflection.

What shall make a life of joy?

Happiness accomplishes a task.
Joy learns the maps and masters the math.

Happiness cares not for borders.
Joy breaks the chains of unlawful orders.

Happiness makes best bets and good guesses.
Joy lets go of regrets and learns lots of lessons.

Happiness yearns to choose.
Joy earns and pursues.

Can you feel the difference?
Can you hear the difference?
Can you smell and taste the difference?
Can you remember an instance?

Peacekeeping

Be brave, misfits.

Save your good hearts.
Dismiss dread and worry.

Depart from history's circus
and do so in a hurry.
Because stardust is a whim away,

debate the ways to shine.

Unshackle your story
revealing the glory
of your divine colors.

Let there be no other choice than

peace.
Send us off with controversy
and cursed with questions,
smiles, laughs,
and mentions of mercy,
stickered with love,
wrapped in forgiveness,
and delivered in a big hug.

Rules of Engagement

Be loving.

Be kind.

Be simple.

Unwind.

Be gentle.

Be slow.

Remember
self-control.

All of us,
what we see,
this distance
between you and me,
is only enclosed
by love

and, what else,

who knows?

Swag

Authenticity is a way of being
whole in feeling,

scene and seeing
as you'd like:

fighting
falling off balance,

hitting the wrong key,
waiting for next spring,

walking the talk,
bringing the change,

being the wonder-
-fully strange

way you are -
scars, hard stops,

whole heart
and all.

Grace

Grace sits
quietly
waiting

to be
received.

COVID Times

Work more,
not less.

Clean and organize
with the best.

Build a new life.
Redecorate the nest.

Consider the possibilities
of what comes next.

Resurrection

We have arisen
with a promise
      of fulfillment through sacrifice,

      a mention of spiritual ascension
      forgiving our many vices,

      answering the ultimate question
      "Why are we forsaken?"

      and undeservedly taken
      to a watering hole
      that nourishes
      our collective soul

      all at once and one sip at a time
      drinking a bottomless cup
of redeeming grace.

Blessings

Pray for a presence.
Pray for the present.
Pray for our President.

Sleigh within your residence, and
be proud of what you represent.

Go. Grieve all these grave matters,
the great lies that have yet to shatter.
While our means yet drive us towards disaster,
we will get by, if only for uncomfortable laughter.

Pray for a posture.
Pray even for the imposters,
the masters and the slaves,
the mighty and the knaves.

Pray for equal power.
Pray for peace over every hour:
to the east and the west,
prayers in all directions would be best.

Resolve

Bless this land.
Bless this town.
Bless the silence
and the sounds.

Bless the beginnings.
Bless the ends.
Bless our certainties
and "It just depends."

Blessed be. Blessed be.
Blessed are you. Blessed is me.

Blessed am I. Blessed are we.
Prayers to all, in all eternity.

R.A.I.N.

recognize the thought that arrives
let go of the steering wheel

allow the thought to drive
wherever the thought goes

note the scenery
the emotions
the sensations
the strains
the plain feeling

floating along
like a cloud
interpreting now

allow rest to arrive
allow the thought to disappear
do not grasp at this thought or the next
rest and pay attention to the depth of each next breadth

investigate the sound of the many nearby spaces
look off into the distance and note something symbolic

nurture the reason this moment matters
silently express gratitude for the reason why
hold onto this gratitude for a while longer

now give the world good energy

now be blessed with good memories

Love

It is a spoken word,
a turn of tune or phrase,
a simplest praise,

a tender touch,
timeless and treasured,
priceless but barely measured,

pleasured by many
yet censored by the hearts of plenty
who do not care to live gently.

It is a devotion
to bleed your emotions
and embrace your scars.

It connects you to a deeper sense of meaning,
a higher sense of purpose,
a greater sense than can be purposed or pursued.

It calls for compassion
at a time when compassion is unfathomable.

It is a shared experience.

Rehearse these words:
Love is the plot line and we are the actors.

Flow

With purpose,
pour out
slowly,

        handling
        the waterfall
        by measuring
        the sips,
        scoping
        the sounds
        of chirping
        birds, the smell of
        fresh earth, the sight of
        a falling sun becoming
        a blissfully mundane moment
        of peace between riots.

Be that demonstration
of waves crashing
into a washing quiet.

Ready

Do not be that fool.
Be a tool,   an instrument of change.
Be a pencil   put to a page.
Be alive   like a sage.

This stage cannot ready itself.
This day was not made only for your health.

Your wealth is not waiting.
There is no answer that ends the debating.

Trust the path you are on is a good one.
You are not yet done doing this thing.
This is not your time for that.

Still, sit
with your daydreams
before they run
from here. Now,

how to live?
How to give?
How to avoid
getting or giving a shivving?

Go off, try,
be a blessing, don't die,
and survive another day
to pursue your "because."

Set

Compose
yourself.

Take a seat
or stand.

Ready the
instrument.

Stay
still.

Stay
steady.

Until the air chills,
chest feels heavy
and eyes stuck,

wait for a motion,
an approval to play,

to unleash a symphony
of you.

Slow Going

Be

like the winter
melting into spring;

like the earth turning
to reveal the stars;

like the sandy shore eroding
and arriving with the tide;

like the wind whispering to the seed
"I will carry you,

                and when the rain arrives
                you will blossom."

Go

Live with soul.
Here and now,

leave shame.
Speak proud.

Ignore that distraction.
Give life to this action.

It's a matter of simple transactions
infused with the discipline to do it again

until a gain is made,
paid in satisfaction.

Let Go

The past approaches,
quickstepping missteps,
begetting regrets, these
things we'd rather
forget. Forgive

what happened;
what did and did not occur;
what they might have done.

Sue or sew
a way to letting go
and letting it be
all yours in the end.

Cherish it,
or the memory will rot.
In between
caring too little and too much,

is caring enough
to stay in touch
with that time
when such and such
went down
along the way.

Redemption Song

Get up. Stand up.
This fight just begins.

Victory is guaranteed
because your grey spirit grins.

On Nyah

Nyah believes that writing is fighting. He began writing poetry and short stories as a teenager, and honed his skills at the University of South Dakota where he earned a double major in English and Political Science. Nyah has experience as a professional grant writer, leveraging his writing talents to raise funds in support of advancing nonprofit missions. In addition to the written word, he is a practiced spoken word poet, and has won competitions in his home state of South Dakota, Iowa, and Florida. He has an appreciation for structural-theory that is pronounced in his poetry, and holds hope that his work might open minds and hearts to the fierce urgency of building a more beloved community. When not writing, Nyah enjoys life with his wife and serves nonprofits that aim to build a racially reconciled world.

www.NyahVanterpool.com
@because.nv

www.ingramcontent.com/pod-product-compliance
Ingram Content Group UK Ltd.
Pitfield, Milton Keynes, MK11 3LW, UK
UKHW021325180426
11947UKWH00017B/1444